JAN 3 1 2008

From Kernel to Corncob

by Ellen Weiss

Children's Press®
A Division of Scholastic Inc.
New York Toronto London Auckland Sydney
Mexico City New Delhi Hong Kong
Danbury, Connecticut

These content vocabulary word builders are for grades 1–2.

Consultant: Emily Yates, Millennium Seed Bank Co-coordinator, Institute for Plant Biology and Conservation, Chicago Botanic Garden, Glencoe, Illinois

Reading Consultant: Cecilia Minden-Cupp, PhD, Early Literacy Consultant and Author, Chapel Hill, North Carolina

Photographs © 2008: Alamy Images: cover background, 5 bottom left, 14, 17 bottom inset, 21 center right (Bill Barksdale/AGStockUSA, Inc.), cover right inset, back cover, 1, 5 top left, 13, 15, 20 right, 21 top, 21 center left (Chuck Franklin), 19 (Richard Levine); Corbis Images: 23 bottom left (Bill Barksdale), 11 (David Frazier), 23 top right (Warren Jacobi), 23 bottom right (Kelly Redinger/Design Pics), 2, 5 bottom right, 17 background, 21 bottom (Tetra Images), cover center inset and left inset, 4 top, 4 bottom right, 5 top right, 6, 9, 12, 20 bottom, 20 top left; Getty Images: 7 (Larry Dale Gordon), 23 top left (Darrell Gulin); Photo Researchers, NY/Andrew Syred: 4 bottom left, 17 top inset.

Book Design: Simonsays Design!
Book Production: The Design Lab

Library of Congress Cataloging-in-Publication Data
Weiss, Ellen, 1949–
From kernel to corncob / by Ellen Weiss.
    p. cm.—(Scholastic news nonfiction readers)
Includes bibliographical references and index.
ISBN-13: 978-0-531-18536-0 (lib. bdg.) 978-0-531-18789-0 (pbk.)
ISBN-10: 0-531-18536-2 (lib. bdg.) 0-531-18789-6 (pbk.)
1. Corn—Juvenile literature. I. Title. II. Series.
SB191.M2W457 2007
633.1'5—dc22   2007009173

Scholastic 1/4/08 $20.00

CONTENTS

WORD HUNT

Look for these words as you read. They will be in **bold**.

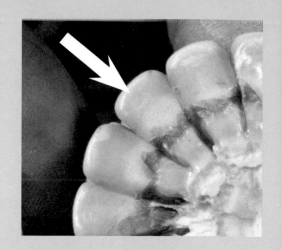

coating
(**koht**-ing)

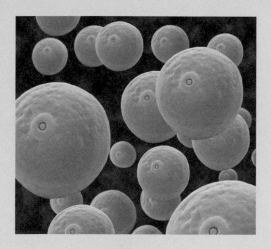

pollen
(**pol**-uhn)

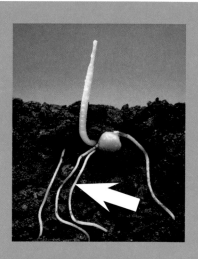

roots
(roots)

husks
(huhsks)

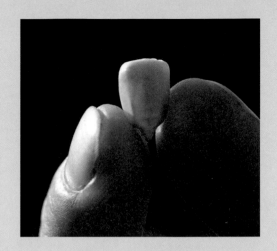

kernel
(**kur**-nuhl)

silks
(silks)

tassel
(**ta**-suhl)

5

Eating Seeds

Yum! Corn on the cob!

Each **kernel** of corn on this cob is a seed. You can eat these seeds.

Did you know that you can also plant these seeds in soil?

Then you can grow your own corn.

kernel

Each kernel of corn has three main parts.

One part is the tiny beginnings of a plant deep inside.

One part is a thick layer of food to help the tiny plant start growing.

The last part is a tough outer **coating** to protect the tiny plant.

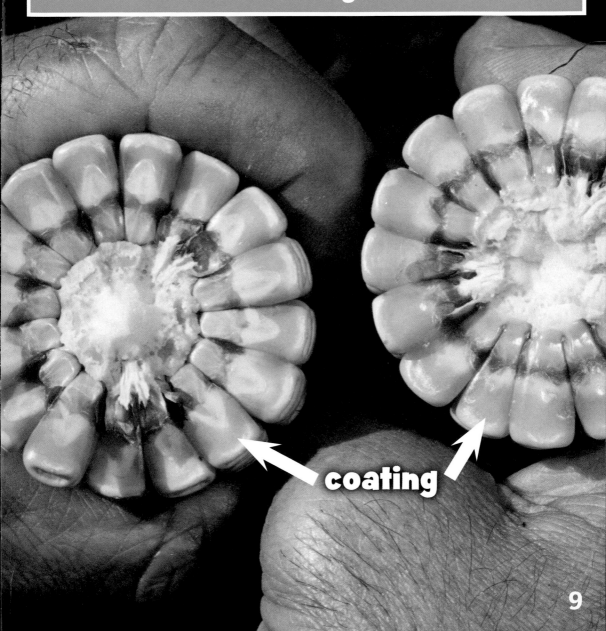

Next time you eat corn on the cob, you can look for the coating on the kernels.

coating

The farmer plants the corn kernels in rows.

The corn plants will need a lot of room.

Seeds need to be about 6 to 12 inches (15 to 30 centimeters) apart.

Soon the seed's tough coating breaks down underground.

The plant starts to grow.

The buckets on this planting machine are filled with corn kernels.

Corn plants grow very quickly. The stems grow about 1 inch (2.5 centimeters) a day!

Underground, the **roots** grow, too. The long roots soak up plenty of water.

The plants grow to be more than 6 feet (2 meters) tall in just ten weeks!

roots

It is easy to get lost in tall corn rows! Never walk into a cornfield without an adult.

A corn plant forms one or two ears of corn.

Special leaves called **husks** protect the ears.

At first, the ears are small.

They don't have any kernels on them.

husks

When you buy corn on the cob, you have to remove the husks before eating the sweet kernels.

A **tassel** grows at the very top of a corn plant.

The tassel has many flowers. The flowers make tiny grains called **pollen**.

Corn **silks** are attached to the growing ear of corn. They look like threads.

Together, the tassel and the silks make something special happen.

tassel

pollen
grains

silks

Pollen from the tassel falls or blows onto the silks.

Now the corn kernels can start to grow.

In a few weeks, the kernels will be fully grown.

The corn will be ready for picking.

Then we can eat more yummy corn on the cob!

You can buy fresh corn
at a farmer's market.

CORN LIFE CYCLE

1 A corn kernel is planted.

2 The corn plant begins to grow.

5 The corn is picked when it is ready to eat!

4 Ears of corn begin to grow.

3 The corn plant grows taller.

YOUR NEW WORDS

coating (**koh**-ting) an outer layer that covers something

husks (huhsks) special leaves that grow around an ear of corn

kernel (**kur**-nuhl) a seed of a corn plant

pollen (**pol**-uhn) tiny, yellow grains made by plants, which are needed for new plants to grow

roots (roots) the parts of plants that grow underground and absorb water

silks (silks) threads that attach to an ear of corn

tassel (**ta**-suhl) the part at the top of a corn plant that produces the pollen

MORE SEEDS THAT YOU EAT

barley
(**bar**-lee)

oats
(ohts)

rice
(rice)

wheat
(weet)

INDEX

FIND OUT MORE

Book:

Nielsen, L. Michelle. *The Biography of Corn*. New York: Crabtree Publishing Company, 2007.

Website:

University of Illinois Extension—The Great Corn Adventure
http://www.urbanext.uiuc.edu/corn/guide.html

MEET THE AUTHOR

Ellen Weiss has received many awards for her books for kids. She has a garden, where she is especially good at growing weeds.